Painting China
and Porcelain

Painting China and Porcelain

Sheila Southwell

BLANDFORD PRESS
Poole   Dorset

First published in the U.K. 1980

Copyright © 1980 Blandford Press, Ltd.,
Link House, West Street,
Poole, Dorset, BH15 1LL

British Library Cataloguing in Publication Data

Southwell, Sheila
    Painting china and porcelain.
    1. China painting
    738.1'5   NK4605

ISBN 0 7137 0992 8

Set in 10 on 11pt V.I.P. Melior
Set, printed and bound in Great Britain by
Fakenham Press Limited
Fakenham, Norfolk

Contents

I would like to dedicate this book to the memory of my dear friend and teacher, Elsie Flaxman, who taught me all I know about the art of china painting.

Acknowledgements

The author wishes to thank Harry Fraser of Potclays, Stoke-on-Trent, for his helpful advice.

Thanks are also due to Podmore & Sons Ltd of Shelton, Stoke-on-Trent, for kindly supplying the photograph on page 25.

The illustration used on the china in Colour Plate 10 is reproduced from the print 'Golden Oriole' by Basil Ede by permission of Royle Publications Ltd.

1
What is China Painting?

*Given a thing of beauty make it still
more beautiful*

China painting is a fine art form achieved by the application of onglaze enamels to glazed china or porcelain. The china is then fired in a kiln, thus making the design absolutely permanent. Many lustres and precious metals are used to give a rich decorative effect. Depth of colour is achieved by applying the paint in soft, thin layers and firing after each application. In this way even the deepest colours take on a soft, delicate tone giving many pieces the appearance of antique china.

China was first made in the country of that name, and the formula for its manufacture was a secret kept by the Chinese for several centuries. It was brought to Europe in the sixteenth century by the Portuguese, and in much greater quantity by the Dutch in the seventeenth century. Its brilliant whiteness and translucency was so admired that European potters strove to discover the secret of making china. They were long misled by believing that porcelain was of a glassy nature and tried to imitate it with a composition of white clay and glass. This artificial porcelain (soft paste) was used in Italy, Spain and France; it was difficult to model and often collapsed in firing. True hard paste porcelain of the oriental type was a mixture of feldspathic china clay (Kaolin – named after the area where it was found) and china stone which combine at a very high temperature.

The first European porcelain was made in Florence in 1575 under the patronage of Francesco de Medici; this was a soft or 'artificial' porcelain. The first true porcelain came later in 1709, made by Meissen in Germany, and was especially good for figure moulding. Meissen's technical secret was guarded so heavily that for forty years no rivals existed except the Vienna factory (founded in 1719), but eventually the mysteries of porcelain-making spread via workmen who had had some contact with Meissen. As the European countries gradually began to produce porcelain, each pottery developed its own ideas, but also, of course, much copying went on. In some potteries the employees were virtual prisoners for fear that their ideas might be poached by other factories. Each factory had its own china painters, and flowers, fruit, insects, landscapes, birds, etc. were, and still are, popular subjects for china painting. Meissen, Derby, Coalport and other famous factories employed noted artists who specialised in either one or more of these subjects. Often, when one part of the design was completed, the porcelain would be passed on to another decorator, to execute the next stage, such as gilding. The piece would then go to another department to be fired. Today the craft china decorator performs all these various processes and learns much in doing so.

Originally, of course, all decorated porcelain was hand-painted, but with the innovation of transfer printing in about 1756, factories were able to produce large quantities by using the new technique. Unfortunately hand-painting was later considered to be too expensive and gradually diminished until today only a small percentage of porcelain is hand-painted. China painting as a hobby is, however, now gaining great popularity, particularly in the USA, Australia and South America, and is gradually being revived again in Great Britain by small groups which are growing in numbers.

The beautiful work of good contemporary china painters is once again finding its way into major art galleries and museums, particularly in the USA and is now being accepted as a fine art by many organisations.

Is china painting an art or a craft? This question is often put to me during lectures. By definition a craft is a process of making things by hand. In a broad sense, the fine arts include music, literature, opera and ballet as well as painting, sculpture and architecture, and the decorative arts. Here the word 'fine' is taken to mean beautiful or aesthetically pleasing. Surely china painting falls into the latter category.

In this book I hope to pass on many 'tried and tested' tips, and will be discussing all aspects of china painting with the beginner especially in mind. I hope that my readers will obtain as much pleasure from the art as I have over the years. With me it is truly a 'labour of love', but be warned: china painting is a most compulsive art form and once hooked you will find yourself wanting to devote more and more time to it.

2
Materials
and Equipment

Here is a list of materials which you will need to start china painting. Those marked with an asterisk, however, are optional if you are a beginner and may be obtained later on. You may find the list of suppliers on page 77 useful.

Onglaze enamels (paints in powdered form)
Mixing medium
Painting medium
Olive oil
Pure turpentine
Stainless steel palette knife
6-inch (15 cm) square white tile
Smaller tile to mix paints on
*Palette with lid
Brushes
Lint-free rags
China pencil
*Tracing paper
*Graphite paper
*Gold, liquid bright and burnishing
*Brushes for gold
Piece of pure silk material
Cotton wool
Small glass jar or egg-cup
Jar to store used turpentine
Wet and dry sandpaper
*Mapping pen
Cotton smock or overall
Kiln, or access to one, is essential

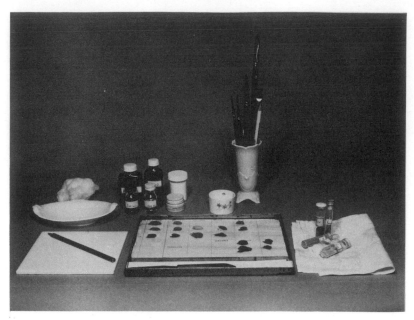

Materials necessary for china painting. Many of the materials may be obtained gradually as you progress in your china painting.

Mediums

Some kind of medium is necessary both to convert the powdered paints into a suitable consistency and also to apply the actual mixed paint to the china or porcelain.

Various types of medium are available, but fat oil is one of the most common and may be purchased ready to use in bottles. It may be made by taking approximately half-a-pint (0.28 litres) of pure spirit of turpentine and allowing it to evaporate in a warm place for a few weeks. It sometimes takes a long time to evaporate sufficiently, so be patient. Always cover the turps with two layers of muslin to keep out the dust.

A good medium may also be made by mixing a little olive oil or oil of cloves with the fat oil to keep it at a workable consistency. If the fat oil is used on its own, it will sometimes dry too quickly and some people may find it a little sticky. It is the first medium which I used and if you do not have a teacher who can obtain an alternative

4

you will probably find that it works quite well for you. You can try experimenting yourself with the various oils available, such as oil of cloves, oil of lavender, glycerine, etc. I even know one person who uses vegetable oil, although I have never tried it myself. Eventually you will discover a favourite.

Balsam of Copaiba is also an excellent medium and here is a recipe you can try: 8 parts of Copaiba Balsam, 1 part oil of cloves, 1 part oil of lavender.

Whichever medium you do use to paint with no trace of it will remain on your completed china, as it will be burnt away during the firing process leaving only the paint which you have applied. The sole purpose of the medium is to allow the paint to be applied to the glazed surface of the china.

Olive Oil

If you use olive oil to grind the powdered paint it must be used sparingly and is best measured with an eye-dropper. If too much mixing medium is used the paint will 'spread' on the china. If too little is used it will 'drag' and not flow properly as it should do. The paint and the medium when mixed should resemble toothpaste in consistency. Paints mixed with olive oil will stay 'open' for weeks, but care should be taken to keep them covered after use. If mixed paints do collect dust and lint, discard them and mix fresh ones.

Pure Spirits of Turpentine

Use only pure spirits of turpentine, and not household turpentine, for cleaning your brushes and for slightly diluting paint on your brush. After use it should be stored in a low, wide container to avoid spills, and may be used several times as the paint sediment will settle at the bottom leaving the turps at the top of the bottle clear. Do not leave it long enough to thicken, however. If you only paint infrequently, throw away the turps each time and start again using only fresh. Turps may be used for cleaning the china prior to painting; wipe over with a slightly moistened cloth and then wipe dry with a lint-free cloth.

China Paints

Onglaze enamels are mineral colours, and are mixed with medium and applied to the china with a sable brush. The eighty or so shades available in the UK may be mixed to give a good colour range, while over two hundred colours are available in the USA. The cadmium/selenium colours should not be mixed with other colours (your supplier's catalogue will explain which are which) or one will eradicate the other. Modern manufacturing techniques ensure excellent colour stability if the china is fired to the correct temperature, and colours are highly resistant to attack by acid, alkali and detergents. Matt china paints are also available.

The oxides most commonly used are iron, cobalt, chrome, antimony, manganese, silver and gold. Gold is used in the manufacture of the blues, and pink and purple colours are more expensive as they contain gold. A few yellows are made with silver and some from chrome; yellows and oranges are also made from antimony. Reds and browns are the iron colours, and red will mature at a lower firing temperature. Manganese is used in conjunction with iron to make some browns and black. All overglaze colours are vitrifiable, and fuse at the correct temperature with the glaze on the china during firing in the kiln. (Firing and kilns will be discussed later in the book.)

It is a good idea to make a test plate of all your colours each time you add to them for your own reference. You will learn which colours fire successfully over each other.

Pen Oil

If you wish to write or draw on your china using a pen instead of a brush, you will need to thin your paint into a pen oil. A good pen oil can be made by taking some of your mixed paint from your palette and adding a little oil of aniseed. The oil should flow from the pen easily, and you should be able to write your name without re-dipping the pen into the oil. If it is too thick add a little turps: if too thin, add more dry paint. A pen mix may also be made from a soft drink such as cola and powdered paint; it should still be of an inky consistency. If you are a beginner you may prefer to sketch your design in ink and then fire it, as it is very easily smudged. Any colours may be added ready for the second firing. Pen oil can be made from any colour of paint and, if larger quantities are needed, it can be stored in small airtight bottles for further use.

China Pencil

Chinagraph pencil is needed to sketch designs on the china, and any marks made with the pencil will disappear in firing.

Palette Knife

A small flexible knife is easier to handle than a large one. Clean the knife with turps after use to avoid rusting.

Brushes

Several different sized sable brushes are needed in order to achieve the various brush strokes.

Two Tiles

Two white ceramic tiles are necessary; one on which to grind the paint, and one to use as a palette if none is available.

Palette

A palette is not essential, but is useful for keeping paints covered when not in use.

Silk

A piece of very finely woven pure silk is necessary for padding backgrounds. The grain must be very fine so that no grain marks are left on the china. After use wash it with warm soapy water and iron out all the creases.

Cotton Wool

A large ball of cotton wool is used together with the silk for padding and dry dusting.

Lint-free Cotton

Used for wiping brushes and cleaning palette.

Wet and Dry Sandpaper

If china is a little rough after firing, a very light rub with fine sandpaper will smooth it effectively. You must be very careful not to scratch the glaze and only the slightest pressure must be used. To make the sandpaper very fine – rub two pieces together before use.

Cotton Smock

To prevent clothing fibres coming in contact with the wet paint.

Kiln

A kiln is used to fire the china, making the design permanent. Thus, access to a kiln is essential.

3
Colour
and Design

Suggested Colours of Onglaze Enamels

Do not get bogged down with too many colours to start off with; just a few will do and you can add to the range gradually. I would suggest the following:

Lemon yellow	Sunshine yellow	Sky blue	Royal blue
Pale green	Dark green	Yellow brown	Purple
Dark brown	Grey	Pink	

You can intermix these colours to obtain more colours, but do not mix the cadmium/selenium colours.

Selecting China to Paint

When selecting china to paint make sure that there are no minute cracks or flaws, as it can be most annoying to spend hours decorating a piece only to notice later that it is damaged! If you do have to buy something that is flawed, make sure that you can conceal the flaws with your decoration. Badly shaped china is not worth wasting your time on.

Sometimes during the firing process tiny black marks will appear. Nothing can be done about this, but do not use any of the same sort again as it usually comes in batches. Sometimes firing at a lower temperature or in the coolest part of the kiln will prevent these marks from occurring, so if you are uncertain do a test fire.

When choosing a vase or a lidded tall object make sure that the piece is level and does not tilt. I once spent hours painting fuchsias on a lidded sugar bowl only to discover after firing that it looked like the leaning tower of Pisa.

Making a Colour Chart

I am not going to specify names of individual colours as different manufacturers have various reference names, but will refer to colours in general terms. I do, however, suggest that you make a test

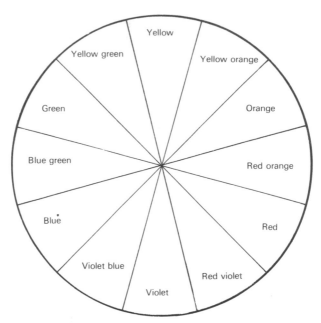

The colour wheel. Opposite colours are complementary to each other.

fire of all your colours on a large plate or tile, naming each one, and making a note of the kiln firing temperature. Also try mixing your colours for testing and make a note of their effects when painted one over another.

It is often thought that colours change drastically after firing, but I have not found this to be true however. Certainly one or two shades may be slightly different on application to the finished colour, but generally most china onglaze enamels change very little. I find that pinks alter the most and may look a little colourless on mixing, but take on a very pretty hue after firing. The appearance of the paint will change during the actual firing process, but when fully fused and cooled the paint should have resumed its normal colour.

Making a Colour Wheel

Colour surrounds us everywhere; in the sky, the sea, the rocks, in fact in everything we see. It adds beauty to our clothes, our food, our homes, and different colours add warmth and tone. For instance if we need a warm colour we choose the red and orange shades. For a cooler effect we use blue or green, and for the light of sunshine we use yellow. The artist can make a sunset by using only three colours – red, yellow and blue. These are the primary colours and by mixing them we get the secondary colours.

We can arrange the artist's colours in a circle to show how they are related. By dividing the circle into three we can insert the primary colours – yellow, blue and red. Between these we can then add the secondary colours – orange, violet and green. Then, between the primary and secondary colours there is still room for six more colours – yellow-orange, red-orange, red-violet, blue-violet, blue-green and yellow-green. These six colours are called the intermediate colours because they lie between the primary and the secondary colours. Any two colours opposite each other on the wheel will complement each other in hue, but added together in equal quantities will produce a grey shade or black.

Colour harmony is the use of combinations of colours to produce a pleasing effect. Colour harmony may be obtained by using adjacent colours on the wheel, but there are no set rules as too many factors are to be considered. Use colours which please you, being careful to avoid a harsh mixture.

Deciding What to Paint

In china painting almost any effect may be obtained and the possibilities are endless, but as the basic china suggests delicacy and beauty the shading is usually kept as subtle as possible; thus floral designs are most popular for this art form. Experimenting with other types of decoration is great fun and should be encouraged. Fruit is particularly beautiful on china, and landscapes give much scope particularly for monochrome paintings (using various shades of one colour). Animals are always popular for children's pieces, and acorns or pine cones and berries also make suitable subjects.

Decide first of all what you are going to feature on your china. Keep the design nicely balanced, and try to visualise the finished piece. Do not be tempted to put on too much as you will have to 'live with the piece' when finished, and once the design is fired it is there to stay. 'If in doubt, leave it out' is a maxim which applies here. You may always add to the design later if you wish, but initially too little is better than too much.

Design

To trace or not to trace, that is the question! There is a lot of controversy among teachers regarding tracing, but bearing in mind that many students will not have done much painting before I would prefer to have a well-executed tracing rather than a badly designed drawing. Do not get into the habit of tracing, though – try to develop and adapt your own ideas; they will come with practice.

If you do wish to trace a design, rub over the tracing paper with oil of lavender to make it more transparent. The design you choose must complement the shape and contour of the china; also it must appear to 'flow' and not look stiff or awkward. Never put large flowers, such as tulips or delphiniums, on small dainty pieces, and conversely wild violets or forget-me-nots on a large vase unless they are arranged in small groups to form an overall design. On tall pieces, such as vases, flowers arranged in an 'S' curve with trailing buds and leaves look attractive. On a large plate a design on the top left side looks well with a smaller design facing it on bottom right.

Well balanced violet design, with the main flowers on the left complemented by the smaller spray of flowers.

12

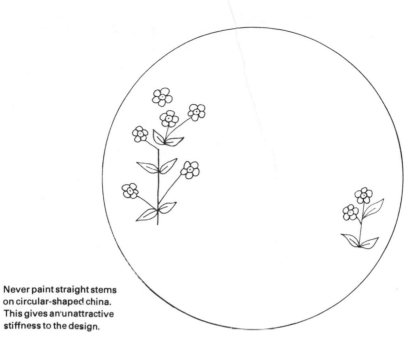

Never paint straight stems
on circular-shaped china.
This gives an unattractive
stiffness to the design.

Correct placement of floral
sprays with nicely curving stems.

Decide which side the light will come from and adjust shading accordingly, keeping the top flowers and leaves lighter and making the under leaves darkest.

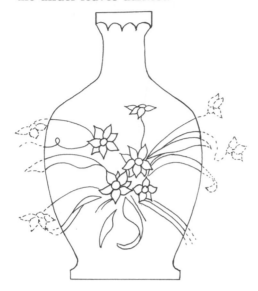

Designs on small pieces should be kept light and airy; here the florets and buds curve around the china.

On larger cylindrical shapes allow the flowers and foliage to 'ramble' right around the piece to give an all over decorative effect.

14

4

Ready
to Start

You have collected all your materials and are now ready to start. Remember always to wash your china before you commence work and before mixing your paints make sure you are in as dust-free an atmosphere as possible and are wearing a cotton or terylene overall. Dust is the biggest menace to the china painter. One of my first mistakes was to go to a lesson wearing an angora sweater. I had to be hastily covered in an old shirt before I could sit in class!

When you are not using your mixed paints put them in a covered box to keep out the dust. If dust is allowed to accumulate on the painted china it will cause the paint to collect around it and leave minute spots which will show up on the piece after it has been fired. The dust, itself, will of course burn away during the firing process, but its evidence will remain to mar the china for ever.

Place a piece of folded cotton or towelling over your lap while painting. This will protect your clothes, and be useful for removing excess paint and turps from your brush. Always keep your working surface clean and uncluttered, and work on a large sheet of polythene if possible. I cannot stress enough how important cleanliness is in china painting if 'muddy' colours are to be avoided.

Work in a good natural light whenever possible. I only use a spotlight when absolutely necessary as I find it distorts the colours.

Mixing the Paints

With a clean palette knife take a small amount of fat oil (or whichever type of oil you decide to use) and place it on a clean tile. Add a small amount of powdered paint and 'grind' to the consistency of toothpaste, no thinner, and continue to mix till all the grains have been eliminated. Some colours, such as pink, may need longer mixing. A tiny amount of olive oil may be added to keep the paint 'open' for a longer period. If too much is added, then add more powder to keep the consistency at the correct level. If your paint is mixed too thinly it will 'spread' on painting; if too thick it

15

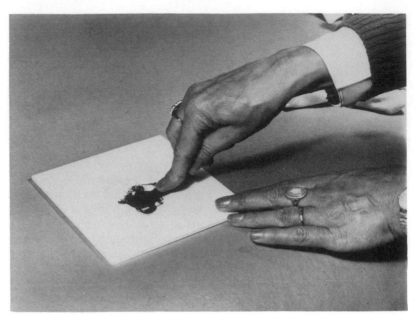

Correct placement of finger on the palette knife while mixing (or grinding) the paint. The knife should be flexible and not too broad.

will 'drag' and be difficult to use. The French and German colours are superb and will grind with very little trouble. A <u>small amount</u> of turps on the brush will sometimes make brush work much easier.

Transfer your mixed colour to your palette. Never be tempted to work from your mixing tile, as cleanliness is of the UTMOST importance in china painting and shortcuts must be avoided. Mix colours in the same sequence each time and lay them out in the same sequence on your palette. This will save you time in the long run as you will always know where to find the exact shade needed.

Clean the knife and tile after mixing each colour. If mixing several colours you may mix a larger amount of fat oil and olive oil on to the tile and take enough to mix each colour from this 'stock-pile'; but never mix too much at a time – it will always be less than you imagine, anyway.

When all the necessary colours have been transferred on to the palette you are ready to start china painting. Keep your palette covered when it is not in use to keep out the dust.

Brushes

Pure sable brushes should always be used for china painting. Initially they are expensive to buy, but with care they will last for years. Never be tempted to buy cheap brushes as you will always be disappointed with the results, for they will not have the resilience and body of fine sable. I always love using new brushes for the first few times as they behave so beautifully and are a real pleasure to work with. At my first lesson I remember I was taught that no matter how tired or late the hour thorough cleaning of the brushes is essential. Firstly wash them gently in turps, then in warm soapy water, and finally dry carefully. I then condition them with a small amount of olive oil in the palm of my hand and thus smoothe the hairs of the brush to a point, before storing them upright in a jar. Treated in this way the brushes will last a long time. Always wash

A few brush strokes showing brush used in various positions.

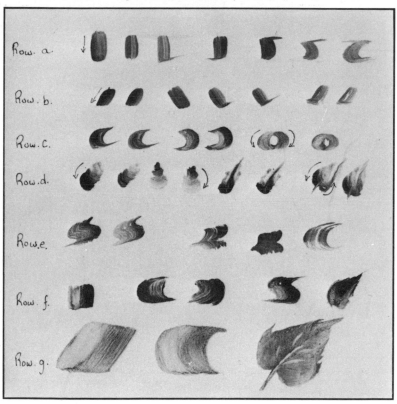

new brushes before use as they may have been stored in a dusty place. If paint is allowed to remain and harden on the brush it will penetrate into the ferrule of the brush and eventually break the hairs. The ends of brushes may be pointed with a pencil sharpener so that they can be used to wipe out stamens, etc.

A lot of attention is paid by some teachers to the learning of brush strokes which I feel is a little confusing to the pupil. I think it is better to practise with a largish brush and get the 'feel' of its possibilities. Try making a 'C' stroke and then do it backwards to achieve different leaf shapes; also try making the strokes with varying degrees of pressure. You will soon learn not to use two strokes where one will do.

Brush strokes used to make a leaf. After painting the initial leaf-forming strokes, use a soft brush to 'pull' them together. Try loading the brush with two shades of green to give naturalistic shading.

18

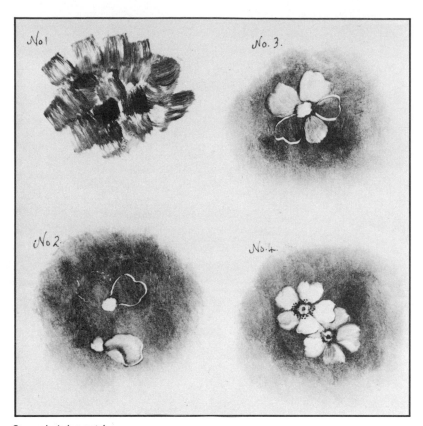

Stages in 'wipe-outs':
1 The brush strokes before being blended together.
2 After blending the background the flower is 'wiped out' with a clean brush adding a 'turn back' on the petal.
3 The complete flower, with five petals forming around the centre. Make sure the petals fit neatly.
4 One flower overlapping another; the one underneath is always darker than the one on top.

5

Backgrounds

For your backgrounds use the largest flat brush you can easily handle. A smaller one will be needed to fill in around the main design. I always cover the entire surface of china leaving hardly any white showing through. This may be done in two ways; either by painting in all the background colours first and then painting the main design, or by painting the design first and firing the piece, and then doing the background on the next fire. I, myself, always use the first method as I find I achieve a more naturalistic effect. However this is a personal preference and you will soon find the method which suits you best.

Apply the paint evenly with long sweeping strokes in the colours you have chosen for the background. Use shades which are complementary to the main design (a little yellow will bring sunlight into the design). When all the background has been brushed on thinly, use a large fluffy brush to blend the colours together. There should be no line between the shades; a subtle, graduated background is what you should be aiming for.

Padded Backgrounds

After applying the colours with a large brush the background may be 'padded' with a ball of cotton wool covered with a layer of pure silk. This will give a lovely smooth background and is always pleasing to do, but make sure the cotton wool is properly covered as it will make a mess if it gets onto the wet paint. If this does happen you must wipe all the paint from the china and start again, as you will never remove all the fibres successfully.

At this stage all the colour should have been applied only lightly. It is better to build up the depth of colour on subsequent firings.

A background put on with a brush will have a higher glaze than a padded one. If you like, you may leave a little white china showing through the background. When you are sure that you have blocked

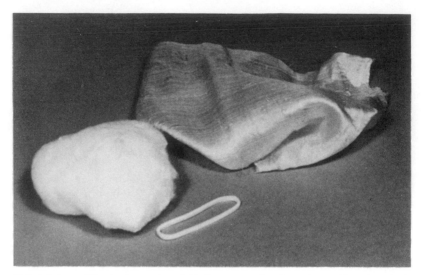

Materials for padding backgrounds: a ball of cotton wool, a piece of pure silk and an elastic band.

The cotton wool pad ready for use.

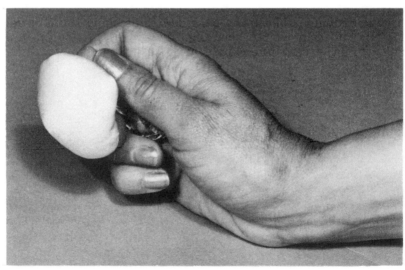

in the background evenly you can lay a wash of paint on the design to wipe out the highlights on the lighter portions of petals and leaves; do not put in any details at this stage, but keep the design light and airy.

Your piece is now ready for its first firing, but before placing it in the kiln examine it from all angles and study it thoroughly. Are you completely happy with it? Look at it through a mirror if you are not quite sure. Make any alterations now if they are needed; once the design has been fired it is there for all time, and if it is not quite right it will constantly annoy you.

If you do not want to fire the piece right away, place it in a covered box to keep dust away from the wet paint – you may put the china in your kitchen oven for thirty minutes at approximately 150 °C to dry it, and then put it into a box till ready for firing. The china should be placed in a cold oven and then brought up to 150 °C. Never put the china straight into a hot oven. If the paint goes a dirty colour do not worry; it happens anyway during firing and will not affect the final colours.

Dry Dusting or Grounding

This is a method of obtaining deeper colouring without having to fire many times. It will take a lot of practice so it is better initially to try it out on flat surfaces such as tiles etc.; you will find the finished effect is well worth the experimentation.

Use a good grounding oil and brush it evenly over the china making sure the whole surface is completely covered. Pad smooth with silk. Put the china in a dust-free box or cupboard and allow it to stand for a while. In the meantime grind a good quantity of paint on a tile with a palette knife till it is extremely fine; an alternative is to sieve through a fine piece of nylon stocking material.

With a clean ball of cotton wool take up as much of the sieved powder as possible and apply it to the oiled china with a rolling motion, being careful not to get any of the cotton wool fibres on the china. If there are any fibres or rough patches after applying the paint the china should be wiped clean and the whole process repeated, as no amount of 'touching up' will do any good and a good colour coverage will not be achieved.

When you are happy with the paint application, blow away any surplus powder, fire at 780 °C, and you will have a lovely, glossy deep-coloured piece in only two firings. The process needs patience and practice to achieve perfection.

DO NOT inhale any powdered paint.

23

'Wipe Out' Designs

As the name implies, the design is 'wiped out' from a wet background with silk over the finger or a clean brush. It is possible to get hundreds of different designs in this way, no two of which are alike, and is an excellent way of using up paint left over at the end of a painting session. Different coloured paint is brushed on to the china using a large brush and keeping the darkest colour where the main design is to be. Pad the colours to eliminate any harsh lines and proceed to wipe flowers out of the background, always pulling the petals towards you. The position of the flowers may be marked out roughly with a sharpened brush handle. When you have wiped out the flowers clean the centres with a pointed rubber pencil. Fire; then after firing strengthen the background where needed and paint in the flower centres etc. Then fire again. Two firings only are needed with this technique as a rule. Monochrome scenes can also be done this way.

6
Kilns and Firing

The Kiln

To me, the firing of the china is a constant source of pleasure and I can hardly wait to see the fired pieces when I open the kiln. It is the culmination of all the previous effort and without it the work would be incomplete and impermanent. Each successive firing is a

A front-loading electric kiln.

new experience and without the understanding of it, one's knowledge of the art of china painting is incomplete.

Firing in the kiln develops the colours and fuses them with the glaze, thus incorporating them with the body of the china. If you can possibly afford it, it is preferable to own your own kiln (see the list of suppliers at the end of the book). Kilns are the most expensive part of china painting, but with correct usage will last for years. This is because the firing temperature necessary is only 800 °C and in overglaze decoration very few noxious gases are emitted during firing. Do not be tempted to buy too small a kiln as you will almost certainly at some time want to fire a large plate or a teapot. A firing chamber approximately 11 in × 11 in × 15 in (28 cm × 28 cm × 38 cm) is a good choice for your first kiln. There is now a small kiln on the market which is reasonably priced and which plugs into a three-pin domestic socket. It is a perfect size for someone practising china painting solely as a hobby and is big enough to fire a 10 in (25 cm) plate with a few smaller items around it.

When you have chosen your kiln it must be correctly placed in a convenient location and wired by a qualified electrician. I have mine in the garage. Space must be left around the kiln for air circulation, and if small children have access to the room where it is sited a kiln-door safety lock is essential.

The kiln should be brushed out from time to time to keep it free from brick particles. All the rules and regulations on safety should be strictly adhered to; these will be listed in the booklet which comes with the kiln.

Firing

Firing the kiln is often surrounded by mystery, but really it is a very simple process when done correctly and you will wonder why you ever thought it complicated. Correct stacking of the kiln is important and it needs a little forethought to get the maximum number of pieces fired each time. As china painters, we are fortunate to have the opportunity to fire our own pieces, as in the commercial potteries the pieces are fired by a separate department after the artists have finished decorating them.

I strongly recommend the use of an automatic pyrometer as opposed to pyrometric cones as it takes all the guesswork out of firing; mine simply has a needle which is set at the desired temperature and which automatically switches off the electricity supply when the temperature is reached. (In the UK a kiln may be wired into a white meter tariff so all my firing is done at night and a 'switch off' device is essential.) If the temperature were allowed to get higher, the paint would eventually burn off the china. Other types of pyrometer have a temperature indicator, but do not switch off automatically.

If pyrometric cones are used to gauge the temperature in the kiln, the number of the cone will determine how long to fire certain colours. I recommend the following temperatures for various colours:

740 °C reds,
750–780 °C all other colours, except gold colours,
780–800 °C pinks, rubies, purples (gold colours).

Of course kilns do vary and you may find that your colours mature at slightly different temperatures. The above are only a rough guide.

If you do use pyrometric cones you may find the following conversion table useful:

Conversion Table for Pyrometric Cones, Bars and Rings

°C	°F	British Cones	Seger Cones	Orton Cones	Holdcroft Bars	Bullers Rings
600	1112	022	022	—	1	—
605	1121	—	—	022	—	—
615	1139	—	—	021	—	—
650	1202	021	021	020	2	—
660	1220	—	—	019	—	—
670	1238	020	020	—	3	—
690	1274	019	019	—	—	—
700	1292	—	—	—	4	—
710	1310	018	018	—	—	—
720	1328	—	—	018	—	—
730	1346	017	017	—	5	—
750	1382	016	016	—	—	—
760	1400	—	—	—	6	—
770	1418	—	—	017	—	—
790	1454	015	015a	—	7	—
795	1463	—	—	016	—	—
805	1481	—	—	015	—	—
810	1490	—	—	—	7a	—
815	1499	014	014a	—	—	—
830	1526	—	—	014	—	—

In the early stages of firing care should be taken to provide good ventilation and to raise the temperature slowly to approximately 400 °C to allow organic constituents to burn away before the colour begins to fuse. You may then put the bung in the vent hole and allow the temperature in the kiln to come up to whatever you require. Do not be alarmed if you look into the kiln and see the paint has turned a horrible brown; this is a natural process and the appearance will change many times during the firing cycle. You should make a test fire of all the colours for your own information and benefit.

The finished, fully matured colours will not look very different from the colours which you applied to the china (except pink), but after firing should have a lovely glazed effect if the firing has been successful. If the colours are dull, or the gold rubs off, or if the pinks are yellowish something has gone amiss; either the kiln temperature was too high or too low. If the firing has not been hot enough, another, hotter, firing will do the trick, but if too much heat has been applied there is little you can do. If I have a diverse mixture of colours to be fired I set the pyrometer at 780 °C as this usually suits most colours quite well, but I always put the reds in the coolest part of the kiln, and the pinks, rubies and purples at the top which is the hottest.

Placing the china in the kiln is called 'stacking' and needs a little thought. If English bone china or soft paste porcelain is to be fired the pieces must not touch, otherwise they will stick together during the firing cycle. If Japanese or hard paste ware is used it is possible to stack the pieces carefully on top of each other or to fire lidded boxes etc. with the lids on, thus allowing more pieces to be fired at once. Do not allow any pieces to come into contact with the elements of the kiln. I have never had anything damaged in my kiln unless the china was damaged or faulty in the first place. Japanese, French and German porcelain can stand a hotter fire than the softer English ware.

Do not expect miracles from your firing. If you put in a badly painted piece you will remove a badly painted piece; and unfortunately a bad design is there for posterity as much as a good one.

My kiln usually takes between four to five hours to reach the desired temperature and when it has done so it should be switched off. NEVER open the door or try to remove pieces while the kiln is still switched on at the mains. It will take several hours to cool down sufficiently before you can unload, but when the kiln has cooled down to approximately 250 °C the door may be opened slightly to complete cooling. When cool the china may be unloaded carefully. The coolest part of the kiln is the bottom, so unload from the base first. If the fired pieces are a little rough to the touch a very light rub with a fine sandpaper will give a nice smooth finish, but very lightly and once only, or you will scratch the glaze. Do not use sandpaper on gold and lustres. To make a really fine sandpaper, rub two pieces together; this will take away any coarse grains and leave a nice fine textured surface which can be used to smooth over the china. Wet and dry sandpaper is ideal.

If you are not lucky enough to own your own kiln, you may be able to get your teacher or another potter to fire for you. Make sure that your china is dry and that there are no dirty finger marks on the unpainted portions. If you are doing the firing for anyone else make sure to point out any nicks or cracks in the china which they may not have noticed, as there is a strong possibility you will be blamed after it has been fired! Quite often little black spots or blisters will appear during the firing. This is because the china was faulty, old or damp (yes, china can sometimes absorb damp) and it is not wise to fire antique pieces before warning the owner that this can happen beforehand. Also, check that you have removed any adhesive labels from the underside of the china.

If you are having the pieces fired for you, remember that stacking and firing the kiln is an expensive and time-consuming procedure so do not expect your china to be fired for nothing. Your teacher will have a scale of charges appropriate to the kiln used.

Be prepared to repeat the painting and firing process till you are happy with the piece. If the paint chips during firing it is because it has been applied too heavily; light applications of colour are what we are striving for. This mistake is usually made once only, as it is so disappointing to see this happen after spending hours painting it! If the paint looks dull or rubs off after firing, it has not been fired hot enough. Refire it at a higher temperature. However, if fired too hot the glaze will be very glossy and the colours distorted, the pinks taking on a reddish tone.

7
Gold
and Silver

Gold

A whole book could be devoted to gold and its application, but I am going to deal only with the basics here. The application of gold is a very important part of china decoration and, provided care is taken and the rules adhered to, it can be tackled safely by the beginner. I, myself, used gold during my fourth lesson and was thrilled and delighted with a 'professional' looking piece. Gold must always be used with discretion, as too much of it will spoil a piece or 'gild the lily' as it were.

Gold comes in several forms, but it is the liquid variety only with which I will deal as it is the most readily available and the easiest to use. It will evaporate quickly, so it is important to replace the lid tightly after use as it is too expensive a commodity to waste. I always anchor my bottle in a large wedge of plasticine to avoid spills, as I can assure you it is a traumatic experience to see an expensive amount of gold spreading over the table. It is a good idea to label the corks on each bottle of precious metal as they all look alike in the bottle. A gold coloured drawing pin stuck in the lid of the bottle containing gold and a silver pin in the silver etc. is a good idea, but only open one bottle at a time to be on the safe side.

Liquid Bright Gold

As the name implies this comes in a liquid form; it is a dark brown colour in its unfired state and is applied to the china in a thin, even coat using a CLEAN BRUSH. When fired the gold will be bright and shiny bearing no resemblance to its unfired state. It need not be applied absolutely evenly as it will even itself out during firing. Two coats must be applied, firing each one separately, or the gold will not be absolutely permanent. When applying the gold be careful not to get any smears where you do not want them, for instance on the underside of the china, or you will be left with a purple smear after firing which can only be removed with a gold eraser.

31

It is advisable to use a separate brush for gold; in fact a different one for each precious metal and lustre is a good idea and a good way of using old brushes no longer any use for painting with.

Gold must not be allowed to come into contact with any unfired colour or you will get a 'muddy' patch on the china. Gold can be successfully applied over a fired colour, but will often give a matt effect which can look very attractive. Do not be tempted to apply the liquid too thickly; any amount used over whatever is necessary for an even coverage is wasteful and can ruin the piece. Remember – two thin layers are better than one thick one.

Another attractive effect can be obtained by using the tip end of a large brush in a 'stippling' motion. Do not use too much liquid decoration on any one piece as too much will often look 'glittery' and vulgar if overdone. It is definitely not a case of 'if a little looks good a lot will look better', so do not be tempted to 'add a bit more' as you will not like the finished effect. Scrollwork may be applied with liquid bright gold using a fine pen.

If applying gold to English bone china do not fire at too high a temperature as it will occasionally 'crackle'; about 780°C will be high enough. Turpentine should never be used to thin gold which has thickened in the bottle: there is a special 'precious metal thinner' available (see the list of suppliers at the end of book). Oil of lavender may be used, but it is expensive. Gold pens are available with a felt tip, and fire exactly the same way as gold paint.

Burnishing Gold (Matt Gold)

This is a liquid applied in the same way as liquid bright gold, but which needs to be burnished after firing with either special burnishing sand or a burnishing rubber purchased for this purpose. After firing the gold will be dull, but after rubbing gently with the burnishing agent it will take on a beautiful antiqued look which you may prefer to the bright gold. Two coats must be applied. As burnishing gold is always more expensive it is quite in order to use liquid bright gold as the first coat and as a base for the second coat of burnished gold, firing each one separately.

Do not touch the gold areas between firings as you may find that finger marks will show.

To use the burnishing sand, moisten a soft cloth with water and dip it lightly into the sand. Then gently buff the gold till it takes on a soft antiqued look, rinse off any surplus sand and dry. It is difficult to achieve a gold line around a plate by hand, so try using a banding wheel. As gold is very expensive for practice use a different colour or a lustre until you have achieved a measure of accuracy. On pieces such as cups and saucers which are used regularly you may find that the gold will wear off in time. This is because it 'sits on top' of the glaze and is not absorbed into it as are the enamel onglaze colours. The gold can be re-applied and fired, however, making the piece as good as new. On cabinet and exhibition pieces which are not handled constantly the gold will last indefinitely.

Silver and Platinum

Silver is warmer in tone than platinum, though both are applied in liquid form in a similar method to gold. Silver can tarnish in use, but a tiny drop of gold mixed with it will prevent tarnishing. Platinum does not tarnish, and is deeper in effect than silver. Two coats should be applied, firing between each, and both silver and platinum will come from the kiln shiny and bright. All-over coats of silver give an appearance resembling silver plate.

Both liquid gold and silver may be applied with a fine pen, especially attractive for lettering.

8
Lustres

Lustres are made from metallic oxides and are applied to the glazed surface of the china to give many different effects. The metal is held in suspension in the liquid and, when fired, the heat dissipates the oxygen destroying the organic matter in the metallic coating and leaving a hard film of lustrous metal. It was applied first to cream ware and earthenware, and later to bone china. This practice was known to early Persian potters, and was much used by them.

Lustres can be used alone as an all-over decoration, or may be applied leaving reserved panels for other types of decoration such as landscape scenes etc. It was particularly popular in the early nineteenth century, and early lustre wares are very much sought after by antique collectors.

Lustres all have one thing in common – their beautiful irridescence. They are available in liquid form in many different colours ready to be used straight from the bottle. If the lustres become too thick they may be thinned with essence of lavender or with a special thinning essence which is available (see the list of suppliers at the end of the book).

Most of the lustres look alike in their bottles, so care should be taken not to get the corks mixed during use. I usually put a colour identification label on the cork and a matching one on the bottle as precautionary measures. The bottles should be well shaken before use to stir up the sediment which may have accumulated at the bottom. If used without shaking, the colours may fire paler than usual.

Dust is the biggest enemy when using lustres as it will leave tiny spots on the fired china where the liquid has accumulated around it. The dust, of course, will burn away during the firing, but the little piles of paint remain as a reminder. Two coats must be applied, firing between each coat; like the gold, lustres sit on top of the glaze.

The liquid lustre should be applied with a large soft CLEAN brush and ideally a different brush should be used for each colour. Brushes should be cleaned in alcohol after use if possible and stored in a dust-free box. The china must be scrupulously clean before applying the liquid and alcohol is the best cleanser for this. Finger marks must not be left on the china or they will fire dull. The damp lustre can be padded with silk to get a pale, even finish, or if a really irridescent effect is required the brush can be 'swirled' on the china; this effect is particularly beautiful with mother-of-pearl lustre. Mistakes on backgrounds can sometimes be rectified by applying mother-of-pearl over the fired colour; in fact, I have used it over fired liquid bright gold which had been applied badly and, to my delight, have obtained a lovely 'petrol' effect with it. Experiment by applying one colour over another for unusual effects, but remember to fire each colour between applications – you will be very happy with some of the results.

The lustres are a little unpredictable in as much as one never quite knows exactly what finish to expect when removing them from the kiln. If matching pieces are required, they must all be painted and fired at the same time, but they will rarely be exactly alike. Many colours are available and some are listed below:

Mother-of-Pearl	Mother-of-pearl is the 'good fairy' of all the lustres. It may be applied over any fired colour to beautiful effect.
Pink	Pink padded with silk achieves a lovely soft warm tone.
Ruby	Ruby must be fired at a high temperature and, used on its own, gives a beautiful tone. With orange used over it, it takes on a scarlet finish. As it is one of the gold colours it will congeal with age so do not buy large quantities of it.
Black	Black needs to be applied two or three times to achieve a deep finish and must have a coat of mother-of-pearl on the top to make it permanent; a beautiful lustre.
Opal	Opal is very pale and delicate, and makes an attractive lining for cups.
Blue	Blue is lovely when padded since it takes on a very delicate tone.
Copper	As the name suggests, this is a lovely warm reddish tone and small pieces painted all over with

copper lustre take on a beautiful patina. An antiqued effect may be obtained by applying liquid bright gold and then after firing covering with one or two coats of copper lustre.

Brown and yellow lustres are also available

Some lustres give off a strong smell (particularly pink), so always work in a well-ventilated room when using them.

Unwanted fired lustre can be removed with a special gold eraser. Don't be afraid to experiment with the colours. Always put pieces in a dust-free place after you have painted them till ready for firing. When firing golds or lustres the kiln door or the chimney should be left open to allow the fumes to evaporate till a temperature of approximately 400°C is reached. You may then seal the kiln.

9
Enamels
and Raised Paste

Enamels

Enamels come in powder or paste form and are used to accentuate flower petals and leaves. I find it a useful medium when the painting looks a little lifeless as it adds a new dimension. The powdered enamel needs to be ground on a tile with a little oil to give a crumbly thick paste (rather like cake icing) making sure that all grainy particles are removed. When it is smooth add a tiny amount of turpentine to make a 'stringy' flowing consistency. You will need to add a touch of turps from time to time to keep it exactly at the right working consistency. If too much turps is used it will 'spread' on the china and fire flat, losing its accentuating highlights. A little powdered colour may be added, but it always fires to give a darker colour than first appears. To apply it to the china I use a very fine pointed brush, but some people find a fine toothpick easier. The pointed end of a brush can also be used if sharpened with a pencil sharpener. This is purely a matter of personal preference.

Pick up a small globule on the end of the brush, let the enamel touch the china and gently pull the enamel into the required shape. If the lines are not as smooth as you would like, clean the brush in turps, wipe dry and then smooth along the edges of the enamel, thinning them to the desired shape to even out the edges.

Jewelling is a method of decoration in which raised paste is used to give the appearance of precious stones. It is particularly attractive on boxes etc., and is applied in little dots over a fired colour; a rich design can be worked in this way to great effect. Turquoise jewelling on a rich ruby background looks most attractive. Gold may be penned around the design after firing. Scrolls and dots are an effective means of decoration in enamelling and raised paste. These can be lightly pencilled in before proceeding with the enamelling.

Raised paste and enamels should be thoroughly dry before firing.

Fire at approximately 750°C. If the enamel chips off it has been incorrectly mixed and applied. Breathing on the mixed paste from time to time will help keep it workable.

Enamel in Paste Form

Paste should be mixed with as much turps as it will absorb on a tile and applied in the same method as the powdered form. It is possible to use thickened enamel to fill in small chips and cracks in china.

Raised Paste

This is used for decorative raised gold work and is sometimes called relief paste. Mix in the same way as enamels. When fired paint over with unfluxed gold, fire again, and then burnish. Never use liquid bright gold over raised paste.

10
Designs
for Beginners

It is encouraging for a beginner to have something completed at the first lesson, but as most pieces need to be painted and fired more than once, I usually ask my pupils to make a decorative tile to use as

This design may be used to test your colours, and if painted on to a tile may be used for a teapot stand. Keep a note of the colours used.

a test chart for all their colours. This is done by mixing a little of each shade and applying to the tile so that colours form a design (see illustration on p. 41). Not only has the pupil tested the colours, but also has something completed straightaway which can be used as a teapot stand etc., though of course the tile has to be fired first. I recommend that a duplicate be done recording the names of the colours for reference.

The next step I would recommend is a monochrome floral design or scene using a favourite colour. Blue, brown or green are fairly safe colours to start with – don't be tempted by the reds or pinks at this stage. Do not be afraid to trace your design on to the china till you become more proficient and confident. The way to trace on a

Simple design using only one colour.

1 Daisy plate after its first firing. At this stage the colouring is still rather pale and delicate.

2 Daisy plate after its second painting and firing, showing how the background has been 'strengthened' to make the flowers more prominent.

3 The detailed part of this plate was done with a fine mapping pen and fired. The colours were then added and the plate was fired six times in all with a little raised enamel.

4 Large tulip bowl. This piece was painted and fired ten times in all. The scrolling and raised enamel was done on the last firing.

5 Lustre ware showing mother-of-pearl, blue, yellow and copper lustres.

6 Selection of miniature pieces.

7 Lemon design platter and sauce
boat.

8 One of a pair of 'Japanese' plates
with grounded backgrounds and
raised paste.

9 The other 'Japanese' plate, making a pair with that shown in Plate
8. These pieces were fired eight
times.

10 'Golden Oriole' painted following
an original by Basil Ede.

11 Pink rose plate using the naturalistic technique with subtle toning background.

12 Yellow wild roses encircling a scene with a village church.

13 Tutankhamun plate. This has two coats of 22 ct gold with mother-of-pearl lustre overlay.

14 Pansy coffee set.

design is as follows. Firstly clean your china, then carefully place your tracing paper over the design chosen using sticking tape to keep it firm. Make sure that you trace accurately with a ballpoint pen or indian ink so it can be clearly seen, being careful not to miss any of the design. Cut away any surplus tracing paper so that it is easy to handle.

Decide where the tracing is to be placed on the china and slip a piece of graphite (carbon) paper under the tracing so that the carbon side is touching the china. Tape the tracing (with the carbon underneath) the china. Now with an empty ballpoint pen or a sharp toothpick go over the tracing carefully, once again not missing any details. Carefully remove the tracing and the graphite paper and you should have the design clearly on the china. If you do not wish to use graphite paper you can go over the tracing on the reverse side with a china pencil, then place the design on to the china (using tape to keep it firm) and again go over the tracing with a sharp point; this will transfer the design easily too. Do not get into the habit of always tracing though – learn to adapt your own ideas and designs; but, as I have said before, a good tracing is better than a bad design if you are a beginner to art.

Do be sure to buy only good quality china, mediums and colours and follow the advice of your teacher. I personally do not believe in mixing my own shades as I feel it is a waste of time mixing say a blue and a lavender when I can buy a beautiful blue/violet already mixed by experts to a perfect formula. Sometimes it is fun to experiment with colours for your own experience, but there are so many lovely colours available to the china painter now, that I always use my colours as they come. I do mix my colours on the brush, however, as I paint and this way all sorts of beautiful subtle combinations are acquired.

Once again I must stress – do not skimp on cheap brushes. Only the best are good enough for this beautiful art form; look after them and they will serve you well. Do not get into the bad habit of letting your colours overlap each other on the palette – keep each colour well away from its neighbour – a clean tidy palette is essential for good clear painting.

It is useful at this stage to learn to apply a wash and to use different degrees and strengths of colour. Try using yellow/brown shades for this exercise. Use your largest flat brush and fill it with medium and turpentine; now load it with paint and apply it in broad strokes to the flat tile; then do another directly underneath and repeat till the tile is covered with paint. Keep practising until you have mastered the technique of even brush strokes so that you

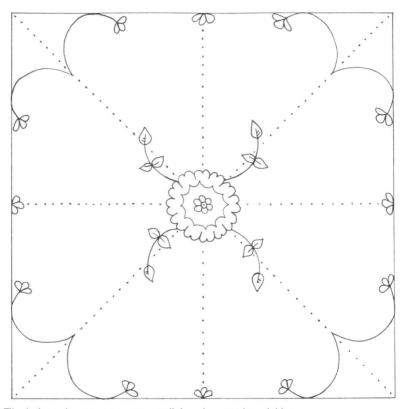

Tile design using a corner pattern to link each one to its neighbour.

cannot see where one ends and another begins. At this point when you have a fairly even background you may like to 'wipe out' a few trees etc. so that you have a scene – this can be achieved in one firing.

While working in monochrome it is fun to do some borders. These look attractive around the rims of plates, cups and tiles, and if several tiles are decorated using a design to link them you can make a very pretty tray or coffee table top. Some designs for borders are shown on the following pages. Practise, experiment and have fun – that's what china painting is all about!

This design is also suitable for painting in one colour. Try blue which would give the effect of a Delft tile.

BORDERS

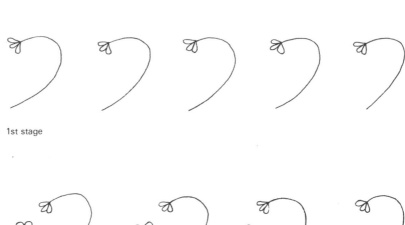

1st stage

2nd stage

3rd stage

4th stage

46

This small design would suit a cup and saucer.

Red poppy design suitable for square tile border.

Forget-me-nots and leaves – another idea for a cup and saucer.

Try small violet sprays around dinner plates.

Try this pattern around a square tray or platter.

11
Ideas for Further Designs

Many teachers recommend beginners to start with wild roses, but I myself found the centres difficult to do at first. I prefer to start my pupils on daisies or 'imagination' flowers with five petals keeping the design simple initially. Nothing is more frustrating for a beginner than to attempt a design which is too fussy or elaborate. Again, I usually recommend working on tiles for the first few lessons as the flat surface is easy to manage and the differently shaped tiles can be put to many uses.

When you feel ready, you can progress to decorating more advanced items. On page 50 I have outlined a project for a plate decorated with daisies which you may wish to follow. Other flowers which a beginner could try are violets, pansies, anemones, poppies etc. – all flowers with an uncomplicated petal formation. Flowers such as roses, carnations, lupins, etc. should be left till you are more accomplished.

Study the turn backs on leaves and petals, and how the shadows fall on the undersides of the folds; you will find that the darkest shadows are always under the lightest areas. Leaves should always appear to be underneath the flowers and not growing out of them.

On pages 52 to 70 you will find step by step instructions for various flower decorations and other designs, followed by a design for a plate inspired by Tutankhamun's treasures.

On no account should a beginner be encouraged to tackle a tea set or dinner service, as it will be a constant reminder of the fact that he, or she, should have waited before attempting such a task.

Flowers of the Month
I am including a list of flowers for each month, as items decorated with the appropriate flower often make really special birthday or anniversary presents which are much appreciated.

| January | Carnation |
| February | Violet |

March	Jonquil
April	Sweet Pea
May	Lily-of-the-Valley
June	Rose
July	Larkspur
August	Gladioli
September	Aster
October	Calendula
November	Chrysanthemum
December	Narcissus

Simple Project Plate – Daisies

For this design I used a fancy edged porcelain plate, but it would look well on a coupe dish.

Colours used

Background – salmon pink, mauve, purple, blue, yellow-green, chartreuse, lemon.

Leaves   – yellow-green, autumn green.

Daisies   – salmon pink wash.

Centres   – yellow, yellow/brown, light red.

1st Fire

Wash in the background with salmon pink, mauve, blue, yellow-green, yellow, chartreuse, keeping the deepest colour where the flowers are to be. Wipe out the centres with a clean brush; then, pulling the petals towards the centre, wipe out each flower starting with the underneath one and leaving the top one until last of all. Leave a little paint on each petal as this will provide shading. Gently 'fluff' the paint on the petals towards the centre. Wipe out the leaves keeping them underneath the daisies. Paint the flower centres in yellow, wiping out a small highlight. Fire.

2nd Fire

Deepen the background underneath the flowers with purple and blue, filling in between the petals with a small brush. Wash a little pink over the petals here and there – not on every one. Deepen the leaves a little, and paint in the stems in light brown. Shade the centre with yellow brown. Fire.

3rd Fire

Deepen the accents where necessary. Put veins in the leaves. Paint a little light red on the centres of the flowers. Sign your name. Fire.

50

4th Fire
Deepen any portion where necessary and fire again, if necessary.

Daisy plate design.

Primroses

Primroses are the harbingers of Spring and should be light, delicate and pretty. The colour of the petals is the palest lemon yellow and the centres are yellow-green surrounded by deeper yellow-gold. Primrose leaves are fleshy with crinkly edges and are grey-green in colour – the centre vein is paler green and is wider at the base of the leaf. The stems are very slightly hairy.

1st Fire

Sketch the design lightly onto china and wash in the leaves with pale grey. Paint the primrose petals with pale lemon and wipe out a few highlights and turnbacks. Paint the centres in pale yellow mixed with yellow green. Paint the calyx in pale grey-green and the stem in very pale red brown. Fire.

2nd Fire

Brush in a little grey background around the design shading here and there with pale lilac. Keep the background colouring light and airy with these flowers. Deepen the petals. The leaves are now washed over with green/grey wiping out the centre vein. Paint in the green highlights around the centre and the tiny circles with a small brush. Paint the deeper yellow centre, pulling the paint out into points. Shade the calyx with green and wash pale green over the stems wiping highlights out on the top side. Paint in the tiny hairs on the leaves in brown extremely lightly. Fire.

3rd Fire

Strengthen background and deepen design if necessary. Fire.

Primroses Step by Step

1 The extreme centre is made up of little yellow-green flat circular buttons surrounded by an area of deep yellow.
2 Petals have a 'dip' in the outer edge and are palest lemon. Each flower has five petals.
3 Leaves are large and crinkly with a widening central vein, and grow straight out of the ground from a little root.
4 The deep yellow centre is pointed in five parts.
5 Calyx showing half open floret.
6 Calyx showing half closed floret.
7 Sometimes the flower stems are very short allowing only the flower to be seen with no stem.

PRIMROSES

1

2

3

pale yellow

green

deep yellow

4

5

6

7

Wild Violets

The violet is one of our best loved flowers and a favourite subject of the china painter. The violet is best wiped out of a wet background. The plate may be given a delicately toned background and fired before attempting to do the design. If you use this method paint the background in very pale mauves, blues, pinks, greens, lemons – all of these colours will look well with violets; keep the colours palest where you intend to place the violet flowers. Pad the background with silk to get a smooth base.

1st Fire

Sketch in the main design, painting the leaves first with pale green; then bring the violets over the leaves and give a wash of pale mauve. Wipe out highlights on flowers and leaves. Fire.

2nd Fire

Filter in background colours using dark mauve and a little ruby under the main design filtered with mid-green and a little blue. Don't forget a little lemon yellow to add sunshine to the design. Deepen the violets and leaves and add the yellow centre. Add a little yellow-brown to the leaves to give them warmth. Wipe out highlights on petals and leaves. Add the delicate stems. Fire.

3rd Fire

Strengthen background where needed, suggesting distant flowers and leaves. Paint the whiskers on the flowers in purple. Add any depth of colour where needed on flowers and leaves. Fire.

Wild Violets Step By Step

1 Upside down 'V' forms centre of flower.
2/3 First paint the larger bottom leaf, then the two 'ears'. Petals 4 and 5 will then fit in quite easily.
4 Stems are very delicate and 'wavy', flowers only part open.
5/6 Paint the main flower first and fit in the others around it.
7 Common English wild violet leaf.
8 Elongated heath violet leaf.
9 Flower wiped out of leaf.

WILD VIOLETS

Pansies

Pansies, like the violet, are a much loved flower and come in a multitude of colours. The make up of the pansy is, I always think, similar to the violet except that the petals are 'fatter' and they have two extra back petals. You can use any colour combination that you choose, but do not introduce too many colours into any one study. The leaves are a nice fresh green; I always paint the whiskers in purple-brown.

1st Fire

Sketch your main design on to the china and filter in the background colour around it using shades of purple, mauve, yellow, yellow/green, and browns. Wash pale colour over the pansies keeping it clear and light. The flowers can be either all one shade or, if using two shades, remember that the two petals at the back are always the same colour and the three forward petals are the same colour. Suggested colours are violet, purple, brown, yellow, orange, blue or white. At this stage wipe out highlights on petals and turnbacks. Wash over leaves with yellow-green and blue-green. Wipe out two small areas at the flower centre. Fire.

2nd Fire

The centre triangle is yellow with grey shading at the top; I sometimes add a dot of red here, deepen the background around the main design and add more colour to the flowers and leaves. Add stems at this stage, keeping them delicate and 'curvy'. Fire.

3rd Fire

Add 'whiskers'; this will give your pansy its 'face' and will bring the flowers alive. Keep the whiskers crisp and clear. Strengthen any other area. Fire.

Pansies Step By Step

1 Upturned 'V' with dot in centre forms the nucleus of flower.
2 Start with large base petal and add petals 2 and 3.
3 Fill in two back petals.
4 Pansy with turned back petals and 'whiskers'.
5 Bud with 2 base leaves.
6 Leaves in groups.
7 Leaf alone.

PANSIES

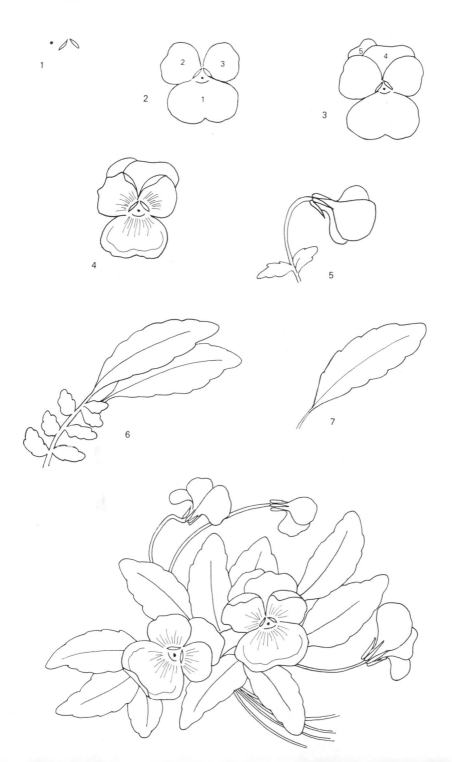

Acorns

The English oak is a design in which all the lovely autumn hues can be used ranging through the greens, yellows, reds and brown with touches of blue and orange. The acorns are green or yellow-brown, the cups green or brown.

1st Fire

Sketch the leaves and acorns on to the china. Wash over the leaves with any of the above colours and lightly paint in the acorn cups and fruits. Filter in the background in yellow and yellow-brown. Paint the stems. Fire.

2nd Fire

Deepen the background around the design suggesting shadow leaves in the wet paint. Shade the acorns and put in the little pip at the end in dark brown. Add more paint to the stems. Fire.

3rd Fire

Add dark background under main design and shade leaves putting in any veins. I like to add a touch of red to the leaves at the edges, but not on them all. A touch of blood red in the background at this stage will add warmth to the design.

Acorns Step By Step

1 The Acorn in its cup.
2 The empty cup – the outside is rough and slightly curly while the inside is smooth.
3 Acorns on the stem – they usually grow in little groups.
4 Oak leaves. Note the curvy edges – a lovely shape to draw and paint.

ACORNS

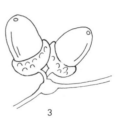

1

2

3

5

4

Fuchsias

1st Fire

When painting fuchsias it is advisable to wait to wash in the background until the second fire. Lightly sketch flowers and leaves on to china and paint the leaves in water green (blue-green) and light green. Wash in the 'wings' of the flowers with pink or blood-red wiping out highlights. The bud is blue-green. The 'skirt' of the flower can be either lilac or white. If you are using white, wash over the 'skirt' with pale blue or water green and then wipe most of the colour off, shading it to give greyish shadows. Do not paint the stems or stamens yet. Fire.

2nd Fire

Wash in a background of pastel shades. Accent the leaf shadows and flowers. Paint in stamens with blood-red or ruby, wiping out the tips with a cotton wool bud. Paint in the stems into the wet background. Fire.

3rd Fire

Deepen the accents on the background and flowers. Put a little yellow on some petals and a little colour on the stamens.

Fuchsias Step By Step

1 The fuchsia bud is composed of three elongated circles starting with the smallest at the top. The top one is green, the middle and lower ones are pink or purple; the lower one will form the 'wings' of the flower.
2 The 'wings' are opened out to show the 'skirt' of the flower.
3 The open flower.
4 Leaves of the fuchsia are bright green and grow in groups.
5 The open flower with the stamens which give the flower its delicate grace. The skirt can be in white, lilac, purple, pink, the stamens ruby.

FUCHSIAS

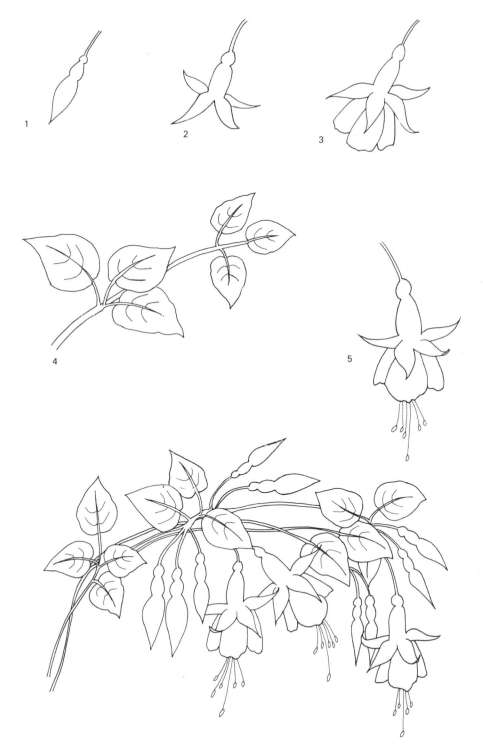

1

2

3

4

5

Poppies

Poppies – bright and beautiful and delightful to paint. I like them best of all on wall plates, with a yellow-gold and blue-green background lightly washed on and softly blended with a large fluffy brush. Add a little salmon pink here and there. Always use a clean brush for red.

1st Fire

Sketch or trace the flowers and leaves on to the china and lay on a flat wash of yellow-red shaded with a little ruby; the flower underneath is darkest. Lay in the background using brown-green under the main flowers. Wipe out the leaves and wash them with blue-green to suggest the veins. Paint the buds with a blue-green centre with the highlights wiped out. Wipe out the stems. Fire. Do not overfire red or it will lose its colour.

2nd Fire

Deepen the background under the flowers with more brown-green and deepen the petal shading. Add a little darker green to the lower portion of the centre disc. Shade the leaves with more blue-green and a little gold-brown. Add more colour to the stems and buds and add the 'hairs'. Fire.

3rd Fire

Deepen any colour where necessary. Remember to keep your brush clean when using red. Wash some petals over with pale yellow here and there.

Poppies Step By Step

1 The centre is pale blue-green.
2 Irregular wavy petals are bright red.
3 Flower showing dozens of black stamens which give the poppy its main characteristic.
4/5 Half flower and leaves which are blue-green and hairy.
6 Poppy bud is blue-green with hairs on the outside; the stem is also hairy.

POPPIES

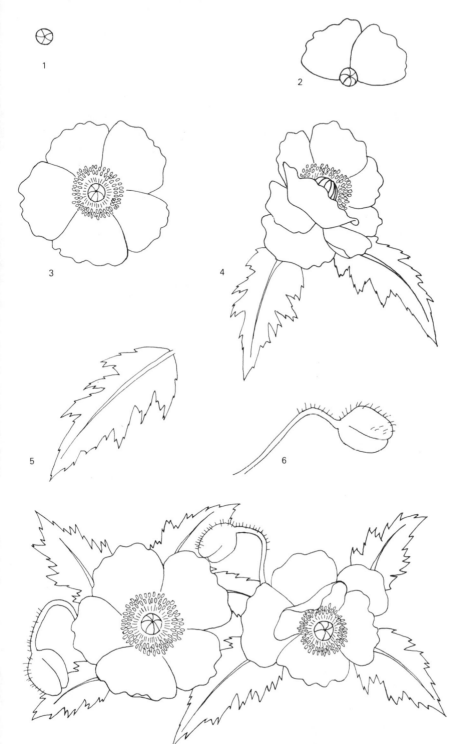

1

2

3

4

5

6

Trilliums

The trillium is a white woodland flower and one which I like to paint out of a dark wet background. Its wavy petals are easily wiped out with a turps-cleansed brush, and make a nice two-colour study. I like to paint mine in dark green and brown.

1st Fire

Brush in the background with dark brown and green. Do not pad, but filter the colours together with a large fluffy brush leaving some texture in the background. With a sharpened toothpick 'draw' the flowers where you want them and wipe out your leaves with a clean brush; keep the leaves wavy and elongated in shape and keep them under the flowers. Now wipe out the three-petalled flowers with silk over your finger and then neaten the flower edges with a brush. Lightly blend any remaining colour on the flowers to form shadows on the petals and wipe out the stamens making some of them curly. Fire.

2nd Fire

Deepen the background colour and wash over the leaves with a little blue-green and add a little yellow-green to the leaf edges. Strengthen the flower shadows with pale grey-green here and there. Paint in yellow and yellow-red stamens, adding a touch of very dark green to the centre shadows. Fire.

3rd Fire

Lightly wash random petals with palest lemon and paint in dark green leaf veins. Add any necessary detail to the centres. Fire.

Trilliums Step By Step

1 Centre of flower is deep with curving stamens.
2 Wavy and curling petals are pointed at the end.
3/4 Petals are always in threes.
The trillium leaf is very similar in shape to the petal and can be lighter in colour at the edges. Keep the background dark in value.

TRILLIUMS

1

2

3

4

Wild Roses

William Shakespeare refers to the wild rose as Eglantine or Sweet Briar. These names suggest the delicate beauty of the wild rose which is the palest pink. The leaves of the wild rose are arranged in threes and fives and can make a very pretty study even without the flowers. The essence of painting this flower is to keep the colouring very delicate. The leaves look well if a touch of blue is added. The centre of the rose is soft yellow with a highlight wiped out.

1st Fire

Sketch in the design lightly and give the flower petals a wash of palest pink using a little light ruby to give the shadows under the turnbacks etc. Wash in the leaves with a little yellow-green and shading with some blue (but not too much). Brush in the background using pinks, greys, blues and a touch of yellow. Paint the flower centre in pale yellow and shade around it with pale green and yellow brown. Wipe out the stamens and highlights on the petals. Fire.

2nd Fire

Accent the flowers. Strengthen the shadows behind the flowers with olive green and grey-blue with ruby in the deepest shadows. Add the stems. Paint in more colour on the leaves, wiping out the highlights. Filter in any deeper background colour, keeping the tones deepest under the main design. Paint on some stamens in deep brown. Fire.

3rd Fire

Sign your name and deepen any accents where needed.

Wild Roses Step By Step

1 Centre of rose is pale yellow with outer circle in shades of yellow, green, yellow-brown.
2 The five petals all come together neatly in the centre; some petals will overlap each other.
3 Leaves behind the petal are partly in shadow.
4 Stamens which come centrally to the 'button' in the centre can be wiped out of paint with cotton wool on a toothpick.
5/6 Leaf of rose is a 'fat' leaf. Leaves are in threes and fives.
7 Turnback on leaf.
8 Bud.
9 Downward facing half-open flower.

For a spray of wild roses add shadows under the main flowers and leaves. The background colour filtered around the design may show one or two shadow leaves not clearly defined.

WILD ROSES

Leaves

Leaves – now the imagination may run riot with hundreds of varieties of shapes and shades just waiting to be painted. All the different hues of green, brown, orange, yellow and red are used for leaves in all their glory. Leaves are a vital part of any floral design and must be well placed; many pieces are ruined by badly balanced leaves which have just been painted in as an afterthought. Study your flower and make sure that you use the correct shaped leaf – for instance, do not put a violet leaf with a daisy. Do not overwork the leaf, but keep it light except where in deep shadow, using as few strokes as possible. Stems too are important and should be carefully studied before painting on to china.

Make a study plate gently weaving together all the varieties you wish. Try not to make any one portion of the plate too heavy with design, but keep the balance even.

A useful idea is to paint a set of mugs, each one to have a different leaf study, perhaps using all fruit leaves or all flower leaves. These make very acceptable gifts and you could show, say, five different leaves, writing the names of each variety on the base of the mug.

LEAF SHAPES

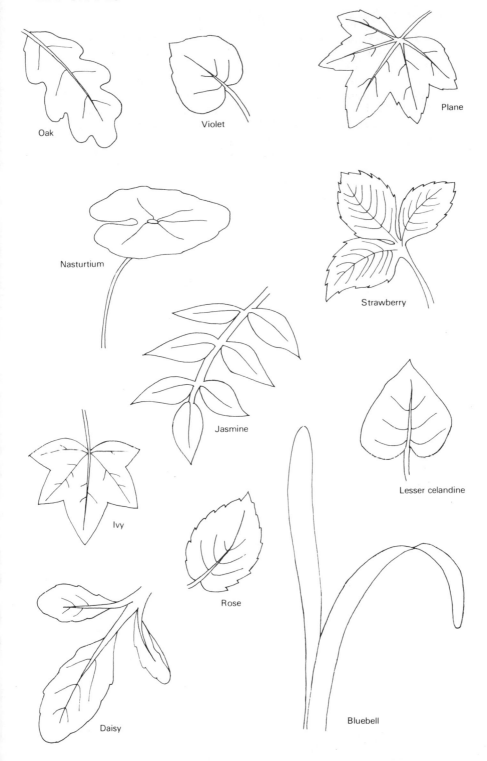

Oak

Violet

Plane

Nasturtium

Strawberry

Jasmine

Ivy

Lesser celandine

Rose

Daisy

Bluebell

Scrolls and Dots

Scrolls are made up of curvy lines in various shapes and sizes. Scrollwork is something which usually frightens beginners, but it is an extremely satisfying technique in which one can become quite proficient with practice. Scrolls can be used as a border in which case keep them simple – small dots can also be added to good effect. Scrolls and dots look most attractive in raised enamel and I like to see gold scrollwork with Dresden flowers. Larger scrolls can make a border for lattice work, a design which particularly enhances small lidded boxes. Scrolls and lattice work look pretty with flowers flowing through them, but the flowers must be kept dainty and not overpower the outline of the curves. They can be made either with a brush or a fine pen.

SCROLLS

'Tutankhamun' Plate

This design took eight firings and includes two coats of 22 ct gold and a layer of mother-of-pearl lustre. I used a rectangular plate, but a round one could be used just as well.

1st Fire

Firstly trace the design on to china using graphite paper. Then, using a fine pen and pen oil, go over the design again carefully keeping the lines clean by starting at the top and working downwards to avoid smudges. You can use a ruler to rest your hand on if you choose. When all the details have been inked in, fire the plate. Do not add any edging design at this stage.

2nd Fire

If you would like to design a border, do it now and ink it in. Fire.

3rd Fire

Fill in the flesh tones and turquoise areas. Fire.

4th Fire

Deepen and shade the flesh areas, and paint the yellow and red shades. Fire.

5th Fire

Deepen the turquoise tones, and add any other colours you would like. Fire.

6th Fire

Cover the entire background with liquid bright gold, being extremely careful to keep the edges clean and not letting the gold overlap the outlined design. Fire.

7th Fire

Apply another coat of gold, and fire.

8th Fire

Cover gold entirely with mother-of-pearl lustre. Fire.

As this plate needs so many firings use only a reliable quality of porcelain.

73

Tested Tips

1 Never work in a dusty atmosphere.
2 Always clean your brushes after use.
3 Keep your working surfaces uncluttered.
4 Mix paints to the consistency of toothpaste.
5 Always keep a separate brush for reds, gold and lustres.
6 Buy the best brushes you can afford.
7 You can pick up an unwanted hair on the wet paint with the point of a wax pencil.
8 Always paint on clean, undamaged china.
9 If using soft English ware, do not let the pieces touch in the kiln or they will stick together.
10 If the pinks look yellowish after firing you have probably not used a high enough temperature.
11 If your colours chip after firing, they were applied too thickly or fired too hot.
12 If your pencil design shows after firing you are not firing hot enough.
13 You may place the painted pieces in your own oven at 150 °C to dry the paint – do not be alarmed if it turns a funny colour as it will right itself during firing at the correct temperature in the kiln.
14 Fat oil can be made by evaporating Spirits of Turpentine.
15 The gold colours (pinks, rubies, violets) need more mixing than the other colours.
16 Make a colour chart of all your colours.
17 A little yellow in the background brings 'sunlight' into a design.
18 Keep the darkest background under the main part of the design.
19 Decide from which side the light is falling and keep shadows in the appropriate places.
20 Backgrounds may be padded with silk for a matt finish.
21 Always work with as large a brush as you can handle.
22 Use grey when shading white flowers.

23 Keep your designs uncomplicated and clean.
24 Follow the contour of the china with the design.
25 Do not eat while handling paints.
26 A dash of violet is a useful colour where white flowers are to be used.
27 Use some of the colours in your main design in the background.
28 A little flux added to your mixed paint will give a 'glossy' effect after firing.
29 Keep finger marks off the areas to be painted with gold or lustres.
30 Fired gold smears can be removed with a gold eraser.
31 Use a mapping pen for gold scrolls.
32 Try a scene in monochrome (all one colour).
33 Golds and lustres 'sit on top' of the glaze; coloured enamels are absorbed into it.
34 Do not let your gold come into contact with any unfired colour.
35 Place your bottle of gold in a wedge of plasticine to avoid spillages.
36 A little gold mixed with silver will prevent tarnishing.
37 Silver looks beautiful with green.
38 To thin gold and silver use a precious metal essence.
39 You may retouch gold on an old piece of china and fire it again.
40 Turps can be re-used if sediment is allowed to settle on the bottom.
41 If your lustres are streaky, a coat of mother-of-pearl over the top works wonders.
42 Too much oil in the raised enamel will cause it to blister.
43 Allow your raised enamel to dry well before firing.
44 Do not blame your teacher for imperfections which appear during firing. They were there before, but could not be seen.
45 A little olive oil will keep your paints open indefinitely.
46 If paint is 'grainy' you have not ground it enough.
47 Keep your ordinary painting brushes separate from your gold brushes.
48 If you rub tracing paper on both sides with lavender oil it will become transparent.
49 Always pull the brush towards you when 'wiping out' flowers.
50 Most of all enjoy your painting.

Suppliers

Kilns and Equipment

Harrison Mayer
Meir
Stoke-on-Trent, Staffs

Pilling Pottery
School Lane
Pilling, Lancs

W. H. Podmore & Sons Ltd
Shelton
Stoke-on-Trent, Staffs

Podmore Ceramics Ltd
105 Minet Road
London SW9 7UH

Potclays (small plug-in kiln)
Brick Kiln Lane
Stoke-on-Trent, Staffs

Wengers Ltd
Stoke-on-Trent, Staffs

Russell Cowan
128 Pacific Highway,
Waitara, Sydney, N.S.W.
Australia

The Little China Shop
120 W. Broadway
Sweetwater 79556, Texas
U.S.A.

General China Painting Materials – Paints, Mediums and Fat Oils etc.

Australia

Australian Silvercraft
   Centre
104 Bathurst Street
Sydney 2000, N.S.W.

Russell Cowan Pty Ltd
128 Pacific Highway
Waitara, Sydney, N.S.W.

The Gilberton Gallery
2–4 Walkerville Terrace
Gilberton, S. Australia

Belgium

Podmore S.A.
35 Avenue Legrande
1050 Brussels

Canada

Joe's Happy Patch
RR1
Bowden, Alberta

Alltrex China Ltd
55 Glen Cameron Road
Thornhill, Toronto

Eva Prokopetz
3103A 31st Avenue
Vernon, B.C.

Denmark

A/S Schjernings Farver,
Ebeltoft

Great Britain

The Art Shop
31 Albert Street
Colne, Lancs.

The China Painting Studio
King's Road
Brentwood, Essex

Rose Art Supplies
7 West Street
Burgess Hill, Sussex

Deancraft Ceramics
  Supplies
15 Westmill Street
Hanley
Stoke-on-Trent, Staffs.

Harrison Mayer
Meir
Stoke-on-Trent, Staffs.

Whitfield & Son Ltd (Gold)
23 Albert Street
Newcastle, Staffs.

Podmore Ceramics Ltd
105 Minet Road
London SW9 7UH

W. H. Podmore & Sons Ltd
Shelton
Stoke-on-Trent, Staffs.

Netherlands

Podmore Nederland
Honore Lambestraat 4
1401 VA Bussum

U.S.A.

Joyce Berlew Studio
RD 3 Moravia
New York 13118

Renaldys
277 Park Street
Troy, Michigan 48084

House of Clay, Inc.
1100 NW 30th
Oklahoma City, Oklahoma
  73118

Maryland China
54 Main Street
Reistertown, Maryland
  21136

The China Cottage
9135 Ohio Avenue
Sun Lakes, Arizona 85224

Elizabeth's China Shop
327 Holly Park Circ.
San Francisco 94110,
  California

Fryhoff's China Studio
9932 W. Broadway
Anaheim 92804, California

The China Cellar
1450 Kingsbury Court
Golden 80401, Colorado

The Little China Shop
120 W. Broadway
Sweetwater 79556, Texas